SF

WITHDRAWN

MENTAL DEVELOPMENT EVALUATION
of the Pediatric Patient

MENTAL DEVELOPMENT EVALUATION
of the Pediatric Patient

By

LAWRENCE C. HARTLAGE, Ph.D.

Assistant Professor of Neurology and Chief
Clinical Psychology Learning Disabilities Unit
Indiana University Medical Center
Indianapolis, Indiana

and

DAVID G. LUCAS, M.A.

Instructor of Neurology and Chief
Psychometry Section Learning Disabilities Unit
Indiana University Medical Center
Indianapolis, Indiana

CHARLES C THOMAS · PUBLISHER

Springfield · Illinois · U.S.A.

Published and Distributed Throughout the World by
CHARLES C THOMAS · PUBLISHER
Bᴀɴɴᴇʀsᴛoɴᴇ Hoᴜsᴇ
301-327 East Lawrence Avenue, Springfield, Illinois, U.S.A.

With THOMAS BOOKS *careful attention is given to all details of*
manufacturing and design. It is the Publisher's desire to present books
that are satisfactory as to their physical qualities and artistic possibilities
and appropriate for their particular use. THOMAS BOOKS *will be true*
to those laws of quality that assure a good name and good will.

Printed in the United States of America
H-2

PREFACE

A PART OF THE evaluation of the pediatric patient typically involves some assessment of his intellectual and psychomotor development, and, if he is of or near school age, some general estimate of either his grasp of academic skills or his comparative readiness to profit from formal instruction. Most pediatricians have developed their own clinical norms for children of varying ages on each of these types of developmental phenomena, because such factors as family socioeconomic level, local neighborhood educational facilities, parental education, and similar general factors may be expected to exert a significant influence on a given child's development in these areas. Even more idiosyncratic factors such as parental aspirations or expectations or the child's family position exert considerable influence, as do such variables as whether the child attended nursery school, kindergarten, or the like. Further weight needs to be given to individual instances wherein the parents, especially the mother, may spend significantly more or less time with a child in activities which might stimulate learning. A college graduate mother who teaches first grade, for example, might be expected to be more attuned to early stimulation activities for her child than a similarly educated mother who is engaged in other types of work.

With consideration given to pertinent unique family variables which can enhance or retard a child's general mental development, there is considerable value to the pediatrician or other physician who works with children in having available more general normative expectancy levels based on a sample of children of given ages from around the country. Such information will not only enable the physician to predict how well a child may be expected to perform in any fairly typical school but will also give the physician some basis for estimating the comparability of the children he sees with other children from other geographic areas.

The items listed for each age do not constitute a test, nor are they

[v]

items which need to be summed to produce any sort of score. Rather, tasks are listed at age levels which reflect when most children can commonly perform these tasks.

In effect, the book presents a series of expectancies or norms for given ages against which the pediatrician can compare the children he sees, in much the same way that he compares a child's heart rate, height, or head circumference against a set of norms or expectancy tables.

LAWRENCE C. HARTLAGE
DAVID G. LUCAS

INTRODUCTION

Eｄｕｃａｔｏｒｓ and parents are increasingly turning to pediatricians for support, help, and guidance with educational matters. Terms such as *dyslexia, hyperkinesis,* and *minimal cerebral dysfunction* are appearing with progressive frequency in educational literature, and parents are turning to pediatricians for answers to questions like, "Do you think Mike's ready to start kindergarten?" or "Do you think summer school would help Mary?"

Many states require pediatric evaluations before assigning children to special classes, and a large number of bewildered teachers and school administrators who are frustrated by an inability to teach certain children are asking pediatricians to help them understand why their best educational efforts have been unproductive. Parents increasingly ask whether medication might accelerate their child's learning, or seek a medical explanation for below average school performance.

In terms of incidence, the percentage of school-age children in academic difficulty is impressive. Recent United States Office of Education figures report that approximately one child of every four is at least one grade below reading expectancy, and the Bureau of Education for the Handicapped estimates that nearly 2 million children may have some specific learning disability. Strictly on the basis of intellectual ability, more than 10 per cent of all children suffer from limitations which make it unlikely that they can succeed in a normal classroom setting.

The pediatrician who attempts to help parents resolve their child's educational difficulties is beset with a plethora of conflicting information, advertisements for various psychological tests, and demands for quick answers from both educators and parents. Unfortunately, there is no single source to which the pediatrician can turn for ready information relevant to mental development milestones, academic readiness indicators, or measures of school achievement.

This volume was developed for use as a reference source for quickly assessing a given child's level of mental development in cognitive, perceptual-motor, language, and academic areas. Designed for use by busy pediatricians, it contains comprehensive screening items which can be used for children from ages two through nine, and it provides guidelines for the use of ancillary personnel for much of the screening process.

Chapter One describes mental milestones for each half-year from ages two through five, and for every year from six through nine. Chapter Two discusses procedures for quickly assessing age-appropriate reading, spelling, and number concepts for children by age levels, from preschool through age nine. Chapter Three describes classification systems used by educators, and discusses criteria for determining whether a child may most profitably be educated in learning disabilities, educable mentally retarded, or other programs. Chapter Four develops a program for involving school and/or office ancillary personnel in the screening process, and Chapter Five provides a detailed, checklist-type mental screening evaluation for the child from two through nine, which was designed to permit fairly comprehensive mental screening in about five minutes by either the pediatrician or his trained assistant.

The Appendices provide quick reference sources for the sorts of information most likely to be of value to the pediatrician in counseling or follow-up activities with the learning disabled child and his parents.

CONTENTS

MENTAL DEVELOPMENT EVALUATION
of the Pediatric Patient

Chapter One

MENTAL DEVELOPMENT MILESTONES FROM AGES TWO TO NINE

During the first two years of life measurement of mental development generally relates rather poorly to the child's long-term intellectual growth, although it is possible to measure some very gross developmental phenomena using procedures such as the Denver, Gessell, or Cattell scales. Beginning at about age two, however, it is possible to begin presenting the child with a number of tasks, to assess how well his mental abilities compare with those of other children his age. The principal advantage of assigning tasks to the child during the routine evaluation is to discover if the child actually *can* do certain things, rather than merely observing to see if he happens to do them during the course of the visit. Some children, for example, may sit meekly during the course of the evaluation and it is useful to find some way of differentiating dullness from mere apathy, fear of strangers, or over-strict parental attitudes toward activity.

The following pages list a number of skills which can be expected in children of ages two through nine. From assessing the tasks a child can and cannot do, it is possible to derive gross but fairly accurate indices of his appropriate mental age level. If it is desirable to convert these approximate age levels into estimated intelligence quotients, the transformation can be quickly made by dividing the child's estimated level of mental functioning by his chronological age and then multiplying this quotient by 100 to eliminate decimals. For example, a child of age seven who is only able to perform mental tasks similar to those performed by a typical five-year-old would have an intelligence quotient of $5/7 \times 100$, or approximately 70, which would suggest that his overall level of intellectual functioning is likely in the lower 5 per cent of the general population or within the borderline retarded range. (For normal distribution of I.Q. scores of the general population see Appendix A.)

GENERAL INTELLECTUAL DEVELOPMENTAL MILESTONES

Age 2

The child at two years of age may be expected to correctly identify prominent parts of his body or to point to appropriate body parts on a picture of a child. On command, the two-year-old can typically point to three or four body parts, typically ones like hair, tummy, mouth, and toes. When shown a reflection of themselves in a mirror, most children at two can identify the reflection as their own. During the examination, they may be expected to spontaneously use two or more words in meaningful sequence, although they will not be likely to use word sequences on command. Typical word sequences used by a normal two-year-old include phrases like, "All gone," "Want drink," or "I want that." He often is able to repeat on command simple words like *kitty* or *puppy,* and sometimes can repeat two-word sequences like *nice baby* or *nice kitty.* He can identify by pointing to clear, uncluttered pictures of items such as a chair, bed, hat, telephone, cup, airplane, key, or car. (Appropriate stimulus pictures for various age groups are presented in Appendix J.) Similarly, he should be able to point to the pieces of office furniture, such as a table or chair, and can often identify the legs of the table by pointing. If a piece of wrapped candy is given to him, the normal two-year-old child can, and almost always will, unwrap it by himself. On command, most children of two can remove their own coats or dresses and may be able to make random scribbles with a crayon, build a tower of three blocks, and walk backward a few steps. Almost all children of two can throw a ball, when requested, and often this is a good task to use when attention appears to be wandering.

Age 2½

By age two-and-a-half, most children can respond to simple commands like, "Come over here" and "Hand me the cup." They can often repeat two digits in correct sequence and should be able to follow an instruction to stack blocks (at least 3 to 4 blocks should be stacked so as to stand independently by the child of this age), especially if an example is provided for him to imitate. More body parts should be recognized by age two-and-a-half, and the child should be able to point now to his hands, eyes, nose, and ears. He may be able to get himself a drink from a faucet unassisted, provided that a cup is made readily available to him, and to dry his hands if he gets them wet during this operation. Usually by this age the child has a preferred hand, although the absence of a lateral preference at this age is not significant. If the pediatrician has available a number of items whose use is probably familiar to the child, most children of two-and-a-half can point to the item described in terms of its function. For example, if the pediatrician lays in front of the child a stethoscope, a reflex hammer, a crayon, a cup, and a nickel, the child should be able to identify by pointing when asked, "Which one do we use to drink with?" "Which one do we use to write with?" and "Which one can we buy things with?" In conversation he may use plurals correctly.

He can stand briefly on one foot and when sitting can often imitate crossing feet at the ankles when instructed, "Watch what I'm doing with my feet. Now you cross your feet like mine." He can, following your example, kick a ball without losing his balance.

Age 3

By three, most children can correctly tell you if they are boys or girls, can give first names, and can repeat three digits. Reflecting on increasing development of eye-hand coordination, the three-year old can copy recognizable versions of both a horizontal line and a circle.

At this age, language is sufficiently mastered that with only a little encouragement, the child will describe a favorite toy, attempt to relate a recent happening, or talk about his siblings or playmates in complete sentences. The breadth of objects which he can recognize consistently has expanded to include pictures of most familiar animals, like cats, dogs, ducks, and birds, and even to many relatively unfamiliar animals, like snakes, horses, lions, goats, and elephants. Further, he can begin to identify a few verbs from pictures and can on command differentiate pictures showing activities like cooking, drinking, carrying, driving, and swimming with near perfect accuracy. The child should be able to respond to a few simple questions related to familiar behaviors, such as providing the noun in response to simple questions like, "What swims?" or "What flies?" and can give the correct verb for questions like, "What does a puppy say?" or "What does a cat say?" At this age, he can also repeat after you simple word sequences like, "See the nice kitty" or "Give me the little ball."

His coordination has progressed to the point where he can use scissors to cut paper, and he is able to wiggle his thumb while holding his hand closed. If he has one, he is probably riding a tricycle skillfully by now. At the termination of the examination, most children can put on their coats without help, and some children may even be able to button their own coats.

Age 3½

At this age the child should readily separate from his mother. The range of skills developed in the period between three and three-and-a-half years of age is fairly wide and marks the emergence of a number of new abilities. At this age the child can usually tell you correctly which of two similar figures (such as circles) is bigger than the other or which is smaller. Also, the concepts of long and short are typically developed by this age, and if you draw two lines, about three and four inches long, respectively, on a sheet of paper, the child can discriminate which is longer or shorter than the other. He has not yet mastered the notion that if one is larger or longer than another, the other object is automatically smaller or shorter; but he can, with fairly high accuracy, consistently discriminate between two objects on the basis of either size or length cues. Many children will be able to tell you both their first and last names.

Some children, especially girls, at three-and-a-half can copy fairly accurately a simple, unelaborated cross, as in the shape of a plus sign. Both boys and girls can often match a few simple colors. Beginning at this age, when instructed to draw a picture of a person, the child can spontaneously produce some very gross representation of the human figure. The human figure attempted by the child of three-and-a-half is almost never recognizable, and the body parts, if differentiated, will probably not bear much spatial relevance to each other and may not even be connected but usually will include several distinct marks or lines. (For more comprehensive examples of the drawings typical of normal children of various ages see Appendix H.) Although the child's drawing skills are relatively undeveloped, he can often describe the person he has drawn and show you the person's face, arms, or legs. His grasp of the location of various body parts is much better than his attempts at drawing them would suggest, and he can often show you the location of his own arm, neck, or knee.

Age 4

With fingers spread wide apart, the child can touch his thumb to each finger in succession. He can hop on one leg, imitate tandem walking, and copy a diagonal line.

He has not only developed a fair level of perceptual and motor skills, but he has also begun to acquire information in meaningful form. For example, he can often answer questions of factual content like, "What is the color of grass?" "What does milk come in?" or "Where does a fish live?" Perhaps of even greater significance, he has begun to understand the nature of opposite analogies and can respond appropriately to questions involving concepts like, "You wear gloves on your hand and shoes on your ————" or "The refrigerator is cold and the stove is ————."

He has sufficient understanding of number concepts to count to two or three and may be able to correctly count the fingers on one hand. He is able to remember increasingly long sentences and can repeat without error sentences of up to seven or eight words in length, such as, "The little boy has a black dog" or "The big dog chased the baby cat."

Beginning at this age, the child begins to understand the "how" and "why" of the world around him and can make reasonable responses to questions like, "Why do we have ears?" or other items familiar to the child. In a similar way, he can begin to make rudimentary attempts to define words in terms of their use. In response to a question like, "What is a spoon?" the four-year-old can respond in terms of its major use, such as, "Something you eat cereal with" or "You stir with it." Words of the level of difficulty of car, house and specific articles of clothing are usually easily within the grasp of the normal four-year-old.

Almost all four-year-old children of average mental development can button their own coats when they leave the pediatrician's office, although sometimes oversolicitous mothers may not give them the opportunity. In the case of an otherwise normal child who cannot perform this simple self-care item, the pediatrician may want to consider suggesting that the mother permit the child a bit more autonomy in this and other self-care matters.

Age 4½

Whereas the child of three can tell you if he is a boy or girl, the child of four-and-a-half has sufficient grasp of language skills and breadth of conceptual ability to correctly finish statements like, "Father is a man and mother is a ————." (Regardless of their occasional accuracy, words like *terror, meanie,* or equivalent terms are not considered correct!) He can deal with similar types of questions phrased in different ways like, "I wake up in the morning and I go to sleep at ————."

He can also identify similarities and differences among pictures, and if you draw four circles and one cross in a row, he can easily identify the one which is different. His memory for words in meaningful sequence has expanded to the point where he can respond adequately to complex commands like, "Take this piece of paper and put it on that table, then bring me the pencil which is on the table and sit down here beside me."

Keeping pace with his memory for words is his memory for unrelated numbers, and he can now correctly repeat up to four numbers in sequence. Grasp of meaningful numbers is even better, and he can probably count all of his fingers or at least up to eight or nine. He understands relationships well enough to answer questions like, "What is a chair made of?" or "What is a dress made of?"

Perceptual and motor skills have progressed to the point where the child can do a good job of copying a square. Attempts to draw a human figure result in much more recognizable productions, and the person drawn by the child at four-and-a-half will include well-integrated details like arms, legs, and head, with attempts sometimes made to represent features like mouth, nose, and hair. He can identify by feeling under a table simple objects like a block, a ball, or crayon and will be able to catch a bounced ball.

He has acquired a good deal more factual information since his last visit and can now tell you answers to questions like, "How many legs does a cat have?" or "From what animal do we get milk?" Although he still will be unable to tie his shoes, he will otherwise dress himself completely without assistance after examination.

Age 5

The child of five has developed many of the skills he will use in beginning his formal education. He has fine motor control sufficient for copying fairly complex figures like an X, and some children this age, especially girls, can copy a triangle. Drawings of a person reflect not only increased motor control but an attention to and awareness of many details. Not only does the human figure begin to show good integration and proportion, but the five-year-old will almost always include all the facial details and hair. Drawing without a model to copy, he can draw a box on command and can also spontaneously draw a picture of a house with windows, doors, and roof, and perhaps even a chimney.

He can now count all of his fingers without error and can begin to solve arithmetic word puzzles like, "If I cut an apple in half, how many pieces will I have?" He will be able to recognize and name a penny, a nickel, and a dime. He can tell you his age in years. If presented with a picture of a simple, familiar design such as a circle, square, or person which has been cut symmetrically in two, he can correctly put the pieces together. He probably can tell you that before you can mail a letter you need to put a stamp on it and can probably give a definition of what the word *letter* means. He may be able to complete sentences which reflect some mental grouping of items, such as, "Candy and ice cream are both good to ————" or "Girls grow up to be women and boys grow up to be ————."

Many children at five understand the notion of primitive justice and social responsibility well enough to know that if they lose or break a friend's toy they should either replace it or give the friend one of their own toys.

A five-year-old can recognize representations of abstractions and can point correctly to pictures which illustrate concepts like fighting, saluting, arguing, or balancing. He may begin to recognize cause and effect relationships well enough to verbalize them and is often able to tell you what you must do in order to make water boil, or that if he cuts his finger he should clean it off and put a bandage on it.

Although he is still not able to tie his shoelaces, he may be able to imitate you if you use a piece of shoestring to tie a single knot around a pencil or someone's finger.

Age 6

At six, the child is able to recognize conceptual differences and can correctly complete such sentences as, "A baby is little; a man is——." He is able to tell the differences in questions like, "What is the difference between steel and glass?" His fund of information has now enlarged to include answers to questions like, "In what kind of store do we buy bread?" Although not all six-year-olds know, many can tell you how many pennies are in a nickel. The six-year-old can give good definitions of words like *swing, orange,* or *eyelash* in response to "What is an *orange*?" or "What does *swing* mean?"

He can categorize items on the basis of shared properties and can give adequate answers to questions like, "How are a coat and a dress alike?" in terms of their both being clothing or things to wear. He also shows an understanding of "why" and can now respond to questions like, "Why do we wear shoes?" or "Why do cars have motors?" He can now repeat without error sentences of up to a dozen words, such as, "Eating too much cake and cookies can give you a bad stomachache" or "Staying up too late at night can make you feel very sleepy."

His grasp of number concepts enables him to use counting for meaningful categorization and when presented with ten or twelve blocks or matchsticks he can, on command, correctly give you three, or eight, or six, or nine. He can copy two spatially integrated figures, and human figure drawings will now include details like fingers, ears, and nostrils, with all parts now in reasonably good proportion. He can balance on one foot for ten seconds or longer, skip, walk backward heel to toe, and ride a bike.

Age 7

At about age seven, although sometimes later for boys, children can begin to recognize right from left. Perhaps related to this sense of directionality, the child can copy a diamond (or kite) and now do a pretty good job of copying a Maltese cross. His human figure drawings now will almost always include a clear representation of clothing, such as a row of buttons, a hat, or a dress. Both arms and legs will be drawn in two dimensions, and the length of the trunk will be greater than its width. His memory is not only sufficient to let him repeat five digits without mistake, but he can now begin to make mental reversals and repeat up to three digits backward. For example, if you tell him to repeat the numbers 5-7-2 backward, he can respond 2-7-5.

He can tell time to the approximate hour and can probably tell you the number of days in a week. Number concepts have passed beyond rote memorizations and he can solve mental arithmetic problems like, "If one piece of candy costs three cents, how much will two pieces of candy cost?" He may know answers to questions like, "What are shoes made of?" or "What are houses made of?" and can give action-related definitions of abstract words like *polite*, and *brave*. His grasp of concepts now lets him answer questions like, "In what way are a penny and a nickel alike?" in terms of their both being money or means of buying things, and he may be able to give reasonable responses to questions like, "Why do people work?"

Age 8

By now the child's mental development has begun to show significant effects of exposure to formal education, and he knows how many months are in a year and can name one or two seasons of the year. He will be able to name the days of the week in proper order and can respond correctly to questions like, "What day of the week comes after Friday?" or "What day of the week comes before Monday?" He can simultaneously handle concepts of *alike* and *different* and answer questions like, "How are a nickel and a dime alike, and how are they different?" He now knows general facts like who discovered America and how many things are in a dozen.

His sense of personal responsibility has increased, and in addition to regularly combing his own hair, he knows that if a child much younger or smaller tries to fight him, the proper course of action is for him to walk away. (The fact that the child of 8 may regularly beat up on a younger sibling is not particularly related to mental development; the important element is that the child *knows* he should not.)

Paralleling the child's increased fund of general knowledge is his expanded grasp of relationships, and he can tell you how a cat and mouse are alike (both animals) or how an apple and a peach are alike (both fruit), in terms of a category in which they both have membership. He can define words like *shovel* and *diamond*, either in terms of a major use or a more abstract classification, like "a tool" or "a valuable jewel." If shown pictures of people clearly registering emotions like joy, fear, or sadness, he can correctly differentiate these emotions on the basis of facial expression cues.

A note of disillusionment is usually present: by this age the child no longer accepts Santa Claus as a real person.

Age 9

The child now has sufficient grasp of number concepts to answer questions like, "If you buy three cents worth of candy and give the clerk ten cents, how much change would you get back?" He can probably give correct answers for amounts of change up to twenty-five cents, at least on the majority of such questions. He can also manipulate numbers in reverse order and by now can repeat four digits reversed.

The ability to construct rhymes has now developed to the point where a child can respond to questions like, "Name three words that rhyme with *hat*" or "Name three words that rhyme with *red*." He can also respond to specific rhyme requirements like, "Name a color that rhymes with *bed*" or "Name an animal that rhymes with *hat*."

The child can also define fairly abstract words like *curiosity, hero,* and *destroy*. A very simple test for word fluency in a nine-year-old child is to instruct him to say any words that he can think of as rapidly as he can think of them. Most children at this age can say approximately two dozen words in one minute. He can remember and retrieve factual information well enough to be able to do tasks like naming all four seasons of the year correctly.

His understanding of responsibility is now sufficiently advanced that if asked what he should do if he saw a train approaching a section of broken track, he should indicate he would try to signal a warning to the train or at least seek the help of someone who could warn the train.

By this age and beyond, human figure drawings are almost always complete in every detail and typically depict the person engaging in some sort of activity or action. After about age nine or ten, however, the child's human figure drawings may be increasingly influenced by nonintellective factors, and so the estimate of general mental development from such drawings must be undertaken with considerable caution.

Chapter Two

EVALUATION OF SCHOOL READINESS AND ACHIEVEMENT

For the child of approximately age five and above, part of the mental development evaluation needs to deal with either his readiness for or progress in some sort of school program. Prior to age five, few programs are offered for children with the exception of private nursery schools. These nursery schools, which sometime accept children as young as age two, vary quite widely in the sorts of experiences they offer, but they generally afford the child several hours a day of supervised peer contact and provide the mother with an equal amount of babysitting. A few nursery school programs are structured around educational procedures, such as the European or American Montessori curriculum, but for most practical purposes it is realistic to consider kindergarten as the child's first formal educational program.

Beginning Kindergarten Readiness

In order to profit from a kindergarten experience the child should be able to pass all or almost all of the mental development items listed for age four-and-a-half and at least a few items at the five-year-old level. The majority of children sent home as being unready for kindergarten placement are considered socially rather than mentally unready; therefore, special emphasis needs to be given to social maturity factors in assessing kindergarten readiness. The five-year-old child who cries during much of the evaluation or who refuses to have his mother leave is probably a high risk child for kindergarten placement, even though his mental readiness levels may be adequate. One very gross, but often useful, index of a child's social readiness for kindergarten lies in the age of children with whom he prefers to play. The five-year-old child who prefers the play company of younger rather than similar age or older children may not possess sufficient self assurance or social independence to successfully interact with kindergarten peers.

By the end of kindergarten, the child is more perceptive of his immediate environment. He tells you his street address, telephone number, father's first name, and father's general line of work. Perceptual motor attainment includes cutting along a straight line with a pair of scissors, skipping, standing on one foot, and coloring within the lines.

If the child has not generally attained these minimal readiness levels for first grade, consideration should be given to repeating kindergarten since these foundations are critical for the more abstract and symbolic concepts required in first grade. It must be stressed that lack of attainment at this level does not predict mental retardation but does reflect slower than usual maturation.

For the child who has not been exposed to a kindergarten experience, perhaps the best predictor of mental readiness for the first grade is the child's overall intellectual maturity, i.e. he should perform all or almost all tasks which a normal child of five can do and perform at least one or two tasks which children of six can do.

A number of mental developmental milestones have particular implications for school performance, and whether or not the child has attended kindergarten, it is good practice to measure the child on these particular milestones. Initial reading success in the first grade is related to the child's ability to recognize the shapes of letters and to put these shapes into meaningful sequence to form words. Accordingly, a child who cannot do a good job of copying designs like a triangle, or an X, or whose human figure drawings do not demonstrate good spatial integration of body details may represent a high risk for adequate first grade performance. Similarly, if the child's grasp of simple number concepts is so poor that he cannot correctly count all (10) of his fingers or tell his age in years, he may well experience considerable difficulty with first grade arithmetic.

FIRST GRADE ACHIEVEMENT
Beginning First Grade Reading

After three months in first grade the typical child can recognize and pronounce such words as *red, come, dog, cat, see,* and *we.* By this time, a child progressing normally in reading can read aloud the following paragraph with only one or two words supplied by the examiner:

I see a ball.
The ball is red.
It is big.
I like to play ball.

Mid-First Grade Reading

At mid-first grade, words such as *tree, father, ask, house, chair,* and *eat* can be read aloud, as can the following paragraph, again with only one or two words supplied by the examiner:

The boy has a dog.
The dog wanted to play.
He wanted to play on the bed.
But the boy said, "No."
Then the dog went away.

Late First Grade Reading

By the end of first grade the average child should be able to read aloud words like *dinner, breakfast, cover, them, please,* and *dark.* A typical paragraph which a child completing first grade can read aloud is:

The children wanted to go fishing.
They were afraid it was going to rain.
But after breakfast the sun came out.
It was a good day for fishing.
Father went fishing with them.

Comprehension may be checked by asking the child to tell you what the story was about in his own words or by asking questions related to the story like, "What did the children want to do?"

Arithmetic

Schools vary greatly on the priority given to the teaching of number concepts in first grade. Generally, however, by the end of first grade the average achiever can add and subtract single digit numbers to ten, i.e. $5 + 4 =$ ___; $8 - 3 =$ ___. He can count orally in rote from 1 to 100 and count orally by 2s, 5s, and 10s to 50. He should now know the value of pennies, nickels, and dimes, correctly responding to questions such as, "How many pennies make a nickel?" or "How many nickels are equal to a dime?" He can tell time to the hour, and many will tell time to the half hour. Most first graders have now been introduced to fractions and can fold and/or cut a piece of paper into halves and fourths. He can also tell the largest of two-digit numbers such as, "Which is larger, 47 or 29?"

Spelling

Spelling is not generally stressed as a specific skill to the extent that reading and arithmetic are in the first grade. By the end of first grade, however, most children can correctly spell all four of the following words: *go, cat, boy, and*. The majority can write a complex sentence from dictation such as, "I saw the big dog." Neatness of printing varies significantly and some children, especially boys, will continue to reverse the *d* and *g* in dog and perhaps write *was* for *saw*. Many, however, will correct these reversals spontaneously if their attention is redirected.

SECOND GRADE ACHIEVEMENT

Reading

By the end of second grade the child can read aloud words such as *does, corner, turkey, strong, quarter,* and *every*. A typical paragraph which a child completing second grade should be able to read aloud is:

> The elephant's trunk is used like a hand. Have you ever watched an elephant eat peanuts? He picks up the nuts with his trunk and puts them in his mouth. This is also the way elephants eat hay and grass. When the elephant gets hot, he cools off by splashing water on his back with his trunk.

Specific comprehension questions appropriate to a child at this grade level might be, "What does the elephant do when he gets hot?" or "How does an elephant eat peanuts?"

Arithmetic

The child should now be adding and subtracting two-digit numbers on paper such as, $23 - 14 = $ ___; and $39 - 22 = $ ___. On verbal request, he should be able to write three-digit numbers, i.e. "Write four hundred and thirty-five." The child should write 435. Most second graders by year's end are able to respond correctly to number questions such as, "Four 2s are __" and Two 3s are __." He can now count orally and write numbers to 500, tell you that 534 is larger that 398, and what fraction is the same as one part of two ($1/2$) or one part of three (1/3). Most second graders can solve this written problem, $9 + 4 = 7 +$ __; or $11 - 4 = 9 -$ __. He should tell time to the closest half hour.

Spelling

Typical spelling proficiency includes the words *cut, cook, night,* and *dress*. Most children can write without error and from dictation the sentence, "The boy had a big cat." Printing is still largely preferred, although some children will now be writing. Writing is typically practiced for the first time in the latter half of second grade Reversals are much less common now, particularly in written work. Reversals in oral reading, i.e. *was* for *saw*, are still rather common but usually spontaneously self-corrected.

THIRD GRADE ACHIEVEMENT

Reading

Reading proficiency has now progressed to the point that reading is expected to be the primary skill used to obtain information. No longer is oral reading taught as a separate skill; silent reading is now being stressed. The child can read without error such words as *toward, troublesome, provide, answer, different,* and *perhaps*. He can read the following paragraph orally or silently with fluency and re-tell what the story was about:

The children went to the zoo on Saturday morning. They saw many different kinds of animals.

They enjoyed the clever monkeys the most. It was interesting to watch them peel oranges and bananas. Then they would quickly pop the fruit into their mouths.

The monkeys chased each other around the cage and up and down the tree in the cage. Sometimes they would escape another monkey by swinging from a tree branch using their strong tails. Perhaps they were playing tag.

Many third grade youngsters with a specific reading disability such as dyslexia may not be able to read the paragraph but can comprehend it in good detail if it is read to them. The dull or dysphasic child, on the other hand, not only cannot read the paragraph aloud but also cannot answer questions about the paragraph if it is read to him.

Arithmetic

Borrowing and carrying in addition and subtraction are now done with ease. Written problems such as $49 + 37 =$ ___; $392 + 719 =$ ___; $283 - 194 =$ ___; and $1432 - 595 =$ ___ are typically solved. The child should be able to write numbers in the thousands in response to a verbal command such as, "Write one thousand and forty-three" (1,043); or "Write two thousand, four hundred and thirty-nine" (2,439).

Multiplication and division are usually introduced early in third grade. By the end of third grade most children have memorized times tables to 5 and many to 10. Therefore, the questions, "What is 5 times 9?" or "What is 6 times 7?" are appropriate. With paper and pencil, the child should correctly solve, 45×9 and 123×6. Likewise, $124 \div 4$ and $413 \div 7$ are typical third grade division problems. Knowledge of fractions now includes adding and subtracting, such as $1/3 + 1/3$ or $3/5 - 1/5$.

He now tells time accurately to the minute, and many can accurately respond to the question, "How many minutes are there in $1\frac{1}{2}$ hours?"

Spelling

The child can now spell words such as *order, peach, watch, grown,* and *enter* without error. A complete sentence such as, "The yellow truck was a funny sight" should be written from dictation without error. Few children continue to print at this age since cursive writing is now required for all children.

When a child fails most of the items at his current grade level, an estimate of his actual school achievement level can be gained by presenting the questions appropriate to lower grade levels to find the grade level at which the child is able to function. Standardized tests are required to sample the more subtle differences in academic achievement above the third grade level.

Chapter Three

EDUCATIONAL IMPLICATIONS OF EXCEPTIONAL MENTAL DEVELOPMENT

THE PUBLIC EDUCATION system was designed to serve the educational needs of the majority of school-age children whose IQ range is from about 90 to 110. In the cases of children with IQ levels above 110, the majority can get along easily in school, because their above average mental endowment enables them to learn new material easily and to retain it well. Such children can typically be expected to earn primarily A's and B's in their academic subjects and for the most part have sufficient intellectual ability to pursue college work.

CHILDREN WITH SUPERIOR MENTAL DEVELOPMENT

The occasional child with an IQ in the extreme upper ranges, such as above 130, is often the delight of his teacher but usually is not challenged at a level near his potential by the typical public school curriculum. For these children, representing about 3 per cent of all children, it is often worthwhile to consider letting the child skip a grade or even two grades in order to keep him challenged. The decision to skip grades does run the risk of placing a bright child with classmates who are physically and socially more mature, and so such a decision ought to include such nonintellective factors as the child's size, temperament, and social development. Other alternatives to the education of extremely bright children can include either private schools or enrichment programs which keep the child in the same class with his age peers but give him additional assignments and/or opportunities for the development of his potential. As a general rule, if the parents of a bright child are willing to forego having a high achieving youngster in favor of having a more "average" child, an unmodified public school program will suffice, although it may not stimulate the child to achieve at the level of which he is capable.

CHILD WITH RETARDED MENTAL DEVELOPMENT

Mental subnormality, on the other hand, poses significant educational problems, and if these problems are not identified and alleviated, can cause considerable personal distress to both the child and his parents. Clearly, the child whose intelligence quotient is below 70 and who is by both professional and legal definition mentally retarded is in need of special educational provisions. Many school systems offer special classes for the mildly retarded (generally for children in the IQ range of 55-70), often in the same building as regular classes. One advantage of such an arrangement is that the mildly retarded child attends the same school as his peers and siblings, rides the same school bus, and thus avoids much of the stigma often associated with mental subnormality. School programs for children in this mildly retarded range are often called EMR classes and refer to the group of children classified by educators as *educable mentally retarded*.

Typical EMR programs are essentially concerned with educating the mildly retarded child to approximately a fourth or fifth grade level of academic proficiency over the span of grade school, concentrating on vocational training in junior high and high school years. The aim of most EMR programs is to prepare the mildly retarded child to be reasonably self-sufficient and independent as an adult, with only moderate guidance and direction from his family or other concerned individuals.

The moderately retarded child, in the IQ range from about 35 to 55, is classified by educators as *trainable mentally retarded* (TMR), and a number of public school systems provide educational programs for such children. Most TMR programs are concerned with teaching self-care skills, such as cleanliness, grooming, and general interpersonal conventions, as well as personal safety habits. No particular academic focus is incorporated into TMR programs, but rather emphasis is on preparing the child to maintain acceptable personal behavior. There is also considerable emphasis on prevocational training in a TMR program, since many moderately retarded individuals can, as adults, do productive work in a sheltered workshop or assist with simple household chores.

Educational or training programs are not generally offered by school systems for severely retarded children. Many county associations for retarded children do offer some sort of structured program for these children, but they are not educational in focus.

DULL NORMAL INTELLECTUAL LEVEL

On a numerical basis, the largest number of mentally exceptional children who experience education problems fall in the IQ range of 80-90. Children in this range are referred to as "dull normal" or "slow learners" and account for about 16 per cent of all school-age children. Such children do not usually qualify for any special educational programs or considerations but are significantly handicapped by their inability to keep up with their age peers in academic pursuits. Even in cases where a child of dull normal intelligence does not become discouraged by his chronic lack of school success and achieving C, D, and failing grades, he will probably have to repeat one or two grades before reaching high school. Once in junior high or high school, the educational needs of such children can usually best be met by some sort of vocationally oriented program. Boys in this IQ range generally find success in high school subjects like manual arts, shop, and similar courses, while girls do fairly well in courses like home economics or in business-oriented courses such as typing, filing, and the like. The prognosis for children of dull normal IQ is not particularly poor once they have managed to complete grade school, since once they have reached or completed high school they can achieve some measure of success in vocational areas which do not require a high level of intellectual functioning. Army induction records, for example, show a high incidence of individuals in the 80-90 IQ range who were doing satisfactory civilian work as bricklayers, carpenters, mechanics, painters, pipefitters, truck drivers, and similar types of occupations.[1, 2, 4] (For more detailed examples of types of occupations commonly held by individuals of varying intellectual levels see Appendix G.)

Aside from counseling parents about reasonable life goal expectancies of children of dull normal intelligence, the pediatrician can be of considerable support to both the dull normal child and his parents in helping them understand their child is not just lazy or could not be expected to earn good grades if he "would just buckle down and try harder." The child of dull normal intellectual ability is especially vulnerable to problems involving poor self-concept and lack of confidence, since in his daily classroom interactions with peers he is consistently found lacking. Good prophylactic counseling to help parents accept what is a reasonable level of academic performance from their slow learning child can go a long way toward alleviating family tensions and preventing feelings of worthlessness on the part of the child.

CHILDREN WITH SPECIAL LEARNING DISABILITIES

Perhaps the greatest challenge and opportunity for early detection and treatment of mental exceptionality lies in the cases of children who have significant learning disabilities, but whose average or above average intellectual abilities cause parents and teachers to overlook their disabilities. Children with such learning disabilities as dyslexia, for example, are often not diagnosed until about the beginning of fourth grade,[3] which means that these children have been exposed to three years of academic frustration and failure before the nature of their problem is understood and appropriate remediation can be initiated. Although the definitive diagnosis of the exact type of learning disability from which a given child may be suffering is probably not within the traditional scope of pediatric training, the pediatrician is often the first to become aware of a child's uneven development of mental abilities and is properly the central figure in coordinating the diagnosis and management of a wide range of specific learning disabilities.

Although the course of physical and mental development is predictably uneven and characterized by intermittent spurts and plateaus, a discrepancy among the development of disparate mental abilities can provide a valuable screening service in learning disabilities. In the child of under five years, for example, a discrepancy of more than a year between two mental development areas may be considered sufficient to raise the question of a potential learning disability. A given youngster of age four-and-a-half, for example, whose verbal and language development is appropriate to his age but whose visuomotor skills involving copying designs, stacking blocks, and the like are below the three-and-a-half-year level may well represent a child who in early school years could have unusual difficulty in learning to print and possibly in the development of initial reading skills. Similarly, a child this age whose fine and gross motor skills are developed to an average level but whose receptive and/or expressive language usage is below that of the normal three-and-a-half-year-old child may be suffering from a mild aphasia, lack of verbal stimulation, or other conditions which could cause him considerable difficulty in profiting from regular classroom experiences in the primary grades.

Above age five, a discrepancy of more than a year and a half among various mental ability levels should be viewed with suspicion. A child of eight, for example, whose reading and arithmetic skills are at the beginning third grade level but whose written spelling and design copying abilities are at about the mid-first grade level (or the 6½-year development level) may possibly be handicapped by some form of construction dyspraxia, dysgraphia, or both.

Children suffering from specific learning disabilities often represent risks for the development of secondary emotional problems, since they cannot understand why they are unable to perform fairly simple academic tasks and suffer considerable frustration and anger over their selective inabilities. Unfortunately, teachers and parents often contribute to the problems of these children, since such children generally can do some academic tasks well and are accused of applying uneven effort or of being resistive. Not uncommonly, these children are referred inappropriately for psychiatric intervention due to a supposed "mental block," presumed stubbornness, or resistance to parental expectations. Although a number of children with specific learning disabilities ultimately do profit from psychiatric intervention, in many cases early recognition of the nature of their problems can obviate the eventual need for psychiatric help.

The alert pediatrician can prevent a good deal of self-doubt and frustration to the child by recognizing the potential basis for uneven school performance and can further provide useful support and guidance to the parents in helping them understand why their child may be doing selectively poor academic work.

Prognostically, the outlook for children with specific learning disabilities is fairly good, provided that early diagnosis of their problems is made and appropriate remediation can be initiated. A few public school systems have good programs for children with specific learning handicaps, and if the child has sufficient general intellectual abilities, college is not precluded. There are a few physicians, for example, who although functionally unable to read due to specific dyslexia, managed to make good grades through college and medical school by means of slight modifications in regular academic procedures.

One possible school modification for the dyslexic child, for example, involves the use of a portable cassette tape recorder with which reading assignments can be prerecorded by parents or older siblings. Using such a procedure, the dyslexic child can attend regular classes with his peers and participate in normal class recitation. At times when the rest of the class is reading a given assignment, the dyslexic child can use a headphone and listen to a recording of what the rest of the children are reading. Resultantly, when the reading period is over and the class discusses the reading topic, the dyslexic child can participate freely. When it comes time for written examinations, the questions can either be presented orally by a school secretary or older child or presented via prerecorded tape.

In a related fashion, if a child is found to be dyspraxic or dysgraphic, he may be allowed to dictate his answers either onto tape or to someone who will write them for him. Daily homework assignments may be handled by having the child recite his answers to a parent or older sibling who can write the answers down for him, so that the child can hand in his own work to the teacher in another's handwriting. If, on the other hand, the child possesses adequate fine motor coordination but is unable to write, the use of a typewriter for "writing" his answers may be indicated.

The examples given are but a few of the modifications which educators can make to meet the educational needs of a learning disabled child. The role of the pediatrician lies not so much in being well versed in remedial procedures as in being sensitized to his role in the early detection of the nature and extent of the problem and in encouraging the parents to seek competent diagnostic evaluation and specific educational recommendations.

Chapter Four

ONGOING MENTAL DEVELOPMENT
ASSESSMENT AND FOLLOW-UP

Mental development assessment at six-month intervals for the years two to five and at yearly intervals from above age five will provide the pediatrician with useful data about a number of factors which enhance or retard each child's mental growth. It will facilitate the evaluation, for example, of the effects of such variables as serious illness, death of a parent, birth of a sibling, a change of babysitters, or a move to a new address on the child's mental development. Further, such regular mental development evaluations will provide valuable diagnostic data for help in determining the approximate age at which mental development began to show signs of arrest or retardation, or when any significant change occurred in the rate of mental growth. The importance of such information in diagnosis of various neuromuscular or central nervous system degenerative diseases, brain tumors, and related medical problems probably requires no elaboration.

The major focus of this book on mental development milestones ends at age nine, since by the time a child has reached this age his rate and tempo of mental development have become fairly well established and barring unforeseen major trauma, illness, or psychological upheavals, may be reasonably expected to continue at essentially the same pace. In almost all cases, if the child is going to experience severe learning problems, these problems will have begun to manifest themselves within the first two or three years of school.

The involvement of the pediatrician with the child does not, of course, terminate at this age; in fact, many parents seek the guidance of the pediatrician well into the child's young adulthood. Not uncommonly, parents turn to the pediatrician for guidance about appropriate educational goals for their children. Such questions as,

[26]

"Do you think Johnny is bright enough to go to college?" or variants of this general theme have probably been presented to most pediatricians. Especially in cases where high achievement-oriented parents are attempting to deny the limitations of a child of normal or mildly subnormal intellectual ability, they are apt to pressure the child's pediatrician for assurance that the child will be able to realize their expectations of him.

Although it is probably unrealistic to predict the likelihood of a child's college success much before he has completed a year or two of high school, there are a few general guidelines regarding overall mental development levels required for given educational or occupational levels which may be of value to the pediatrician in helping a child's parents accept realistic goals. In general, children with IQ levels below 100 should not base too much hope on achieving a college baccalaureate degree. In some cases of good motivation, diligent study habits, and a careful choice of schools, a child whose IQ is below 100 can make it through a junior college program, but plans for a four-year college education for these children are unrealistic.

The typical IQ level found in college students is around 112, and the IQ level of graduating college seniors averages around 114. For graduate level work, even higher levels of mental development are generally required, and it is rare that an individual with an IQ below 120 will successfully complete the level of academic work required for one of the professions. Appendix G lists IQ levels typically found among people working in a number of different occupations and gives some indication of the relationship between intellectual ability and representative vocational levels.

Needless to say, any serious planning for advanced education or vocational choice probably ought to be done only after appropriate vocational, aptitude, interest, temperament, and definitive mental ability evaluations have been conducted by appropriate specialists in this field. Often the family pediatrician is invoked as a court of last resort in cases where recommendations are not accepted by parents, and so in an attempt to provide the pediatrician with a very general overview of the role of the child's mental development in career planning, mention was made of considerations for longer term goals.

SUPPLEMENTARY SOURCES OF HELP

The Pediatrician's Office Personnel

Fortunately for the busy pediatrician, most of the work involved in assessing mental development milestones can be performed by relatively untrained office personnel. The receptionist, for example, can do such preliminary tasks as requesting the child to draw a picture of a person, presenting him with designs to copy, blocks to stack, and related items and then inform the physician of the child's performance for him to evaluate. This will leave the pediatrician time to talk with the child and complete his mental development evaluation to his own satisfaction, without requiring more than a very few minutes spent in actual assessment. Chapter Five presents a series of age-specific mental development milestones in checklist form which can be used by either the pediatrician, a nurse who is accustomed to working with children, or an intelligent office assistant who can be trained to collect the information.

Appendix F lists a few brief screening instruments which can be mastered in a matter of a few minutes by either a nurse or receptionist and which can cast considerable light on the precise strengths and weaknesses of the mental abilities of a given child.

Pediatric Neurology

In some cases involving the determination of specific learning disabilities, it may be advisable to seek consultation from a pediatric neurologist for more comprehensive evaluation of various perceptual, decoding, integrative, and expressive functions which may be involved. Particularly in cases where the possibility of some type of receptive or expressive aphasia, convulsive disorder, or related problem is being considered, the pediatric neurologist can make important suggestions for both the understanding and management of the problem. Unfortunately, there are fewer than two hundred pediatric neurologists practicing in the United States, and unless the pediatrician is practicing in or near a city where a pediatric neurologist is to be found, it may be necessary to turn elsewhere for help.

School System Personnel

Many school systems retain the regular full-time services of a number of specialists in fields which can be of considerable benefit to the pediatrician in his ongoing management of the school-age child, and most of the school specialists will be flattered by the pediatrician's interest in their work and will cooperate in providing him with useful information about his patient.

One who is often overlooked but who is potentially extremely valuable as a resource person for the pediatrician is the school psychometrist. While not all schools have access to a school psychometrist, many school systems of medium size have at least one such specialist on their staff, and larger city school systems may have up to a hundred psychometrists covering their schools. Psychometrists have undergone a minimum of six years of college training, typically involving considerable work in testing mental abilities and academic progress by the use of standardized tests. The psychometrist can provide a good first line of contact between the pediatrician and the child's school system and can be helpful in both summarizing the child's relative academic strengths, weaknesses, and unique problems to the pediatrician and then interpreting the pediatrician's findings back to the child's teacher.

Further, the psychometrist maintains close liaison with other school resource personnel and can help integrate the services of such specialists as the school speech and hearing therapist, reading specialist, and special education teacher who will be working with a given child. Most psychometrists are not trained in assessing the spectrum of mental development in children of preschool ages, but for the child of about seven or eight years and older, they can do a comprehensive job of definitive assessment of a wide range of various aspects of mental development.

Child Psychiatry

In cases where there is a serious question of the child's mental health, deleterious parent-child interaction pattern, or need for psychotherapeutic intervention, the child psychiatrist can frequently provide valuable insights and recommendations. In cases where the pediatrician has good evidence of subnormal mental development, significant learning disability, or other identifiable physical or mental handicap, the child psychiatrist can sometimes provide psychotherapeutic support for the child, since in most of these types of problems there often is a secondary emotional reaction by the child.

Many times the pediatrician can alleviate much of the child's secondary emotional reactions to his problems and frustrations by influencing the school and the child's parents to set more realistic expectations of performance. When the emotional reactions persist, however, the child psychiatrist can help the child improve his self-concept and feelings of self-worth. As in the case with child neurologists, the supply of child psychiatrists is quite limited, and a number of specialists in child psychiatry are limited to dealing with the more emergent psychiatric problems.

Clinical Child Psychology

Clinical child psychologists, most of whom have a Ph.D. degree in clinical psychology representing about eight years of college training in assessment and behavior modification procedures with additional supervised internship experience, can often provide the pediatrician with helpful diagnostic information.

Most clinical child psychologists are relatively skilled in the use of personality assessment, using procedures such as the Rorschach Inkblot Test, Thematic Apperception Test, and similar approaches, and can help the pediatrician assess various aspects of the child's fantasy involving himself, his parents, or his views of school, as well as provide comprehensive evaluations of the child's intellectual, perceptual, and academic skills.

Many clinical child psychologists, sometimes in conjunction with child psychiatrists, offer supportive help to the pediatrician in handling problems like school phobias, prolonged psychogenic enuresis, or other moderate behavior problems which do not require the use of drugs or hospitalization. Some clinical child psychologists are in private practice, but most are employed by medical school departments of pediatrics, neurology, or child psychiatry and are commonly available for consultations either privately or through their respective departments.

Chapter Five

CHECKLIST OF DEVELOPMENTAL MILESTONES BY AGE

AGE 2

Verbal

1. Identification of body parts (receptive)
   Example: "Show me your hair, nose, mouth, eyes, ears." (Child should be able to point to 3 or 4.)
2. Spontaneously use sentences of 2 or 3 words (expressive)
   Example: Want drink; all gone; I want that.
3. Picture identification (receptive)
   Example: "Point to the chair, hat, dog, telephone, cup, key." (Appendix L)
4. Object identification (receptive)
   Example: "Show me the leg on the table."
5. Recognize self in mirror (receptive)
   Example: "Who is that?"
6. Repeat specific words on command (receptive and expressive)
   Example: "Say, nice kitty, or pretty baby."

Nonverbal

1. Unwrap piece of candy
2. Remove coat or dress unassisted
3. Scribble randomly with crayon
4. Walk backward
5. Build tower of 3 cubes
6. Throw ball overhand

AGE 2½

Verbal

1. Follows single command (receptive)
   Example: "Hand me the cup."

[31]

2. Repeats 2 digits (receptive and expressive)
   Example: "Say 1; now say 2 - 9; or 3 - 7."
3. Identification of body parts (receptive)
   Example: Have child point to hair, nose, mouth, eyes, toes, hands. (5 or 6)
4. Identification of objects by function (receptive)
   Example: "Which one do we drink with?" (cup)
   "Which one do we write with?" (crayon)
5. Identification of objects by name (expressive)
   Example: "What is this?" (cup, book)
6. Use plurals correctly in conversation

Nonverbal

1. Stack 4 or 5 cubes
2. Obtains own drink of water with cup
3. Dries own hands
4. Kicks a ball on the floor
5. Balances one one foot for one second
6. Imitates crossing of the feet

AGE 3

Verbal

1. Knows own sex (expressive)
   Example: "Are you a boy or a girl?"
2. Repeats 3 digits (receptive and expressive)
   Example: "Say 1; now say 2-4-7; or 3-6-2."
3. Language fluency (expressive)
   Example: "Tell me about your doll; sister; birthday party."
4. Action identification (receptive)
   Example: "Where is the lady cooking; which one is driving?"
   (Refer to Appendix L)
5. Gives first name (expressive)
6. Identification of familiar objects by use (expressive)
   Example: "Tell me what we eat with."

Nonverbal

1. Copies a Circle

2. Pedals tricycle
3. Put on own coat without help
4. Some can button own coat
5. Copies a horizontal line
6. Balances on each foot 2 seconds

AGE 3½

Verbal

1. Size discrimination (receptive)
   Example: "Which circle is bigger; which block is smaller?"
2. Length discrimination (receptive)
   Example: "Which line is longer; which line is shorter?"
3. Names body parts (expressive)
   Example: Eyes, nose, mouth, legs, feet.
4. Repeats sentence (receptive and expressive)
   Example: "Baby has a little bed."
5. Follows complex command (receptive)
   Example: "Put the paper under the book."
6. Tells first and last name (expressive)

Nonverbal

1. Copy a +
2. Draw a person
   Example: May only indicate a circle for head and lines for legs.
   (Refer to Appendix K for typical age normative drawings)
3. Balances on one foot 5 seconds
4. Separates from mother easily
5. Can match basic colors
6. Can button own coat

AGE 4

Verbal

1. Fund of general information (expressive)
   Example: "What is the color of grass?" (green)
   "Where does a fish live?" (water)

2. Single analogy (expressive)
   Example: "The refrigerator is cold; the stove is ———."
3. Counts fingers on hand (expressive)
4. Repeats sentence (receptive and expressive)
   Example: "The little boy has a black dog."
5. Defines objects by use (expressive)
   Example: "Why do we have ears?"
6. Verbalizes definition (expressive)
   Example: "What is a spoon?"

Nonverbal

1. Button own coat and most other buttons
2. Copies diagonal line \ or /
3. Hops on one leg
4. Tandem walks
5. Touch fingers to thumb in succession
6. Balances on one foot for up to 10 seconds

AGE 4½

Verbal

1. Analogy (expressive)
   Example: "Father is a man; mother is a _____."
   "I wake up in the morning; go to bed at _____."
2. Follows complex command (receptive)
   Example: "Take this paper and put it on the table, then bring me the pencil and sit down beside me."
3. Repeats 4 digits (receptive and expressive)
4. Counts to 8 or 9 (expressive)
5. Verbal number concepts (expressive)
   Example: "How many legs does a cat have?"
6. Fund of general information (expressive)
   Example: "From what animal do we get milk?"

Nonverbal

1. Visual discrimination
   Example: "Which is different?" O O X O
2. Copy a square
   Example: Four clearly defined sides.

3. Draw a person
   Example: Indicates head, arms, legs, mouth, nose, and perhaps
   hair.
4. Dresses self independently with exception of tying shoes
5. Tactile identification
   Example: Identify by feeling under a table a block, ball, scissors,
   penny, crayon.
6. Catch a bounced ball

AGE 5

Verbal

1. Names money (expressive)
   Example: Penny, nickel, dime.
2. Tells age in years (expressive)
3. Sense of social justice (expressive)
   Example: "What should you do if you lose your friend's ball?"
4. Problem solving (expressive)
   Example: "If I cut an apple in half, how many pieces will I
   have?"
   "What must you do to make water boil?"
   "What must you put on a letter before you mail it?"
5. Analogy (expressive)
   Example: "Candy and ice cream are both good to _____."
   "Boys grow up to be men; and girls grow up to be
   _____."
6. Recognizes illustrated abstractions (receptive)
   Example: Correctly points to pictures of action representing
   fighting, saluting, arguing, or balancing. (Appendix
   L)

Nonverbal

1. Copy an ✕
2. Copy a △
3. Draw a person
   Example: Complete with all facial details.
4. Draw a house
   Example: Windows, door, roof, and chimney.

5. Put together a circle or rectangle that has been cut in two
6. Can tie a simple bow in imitation

AGE 6

Verbal

1. Recognizes conceptual differences (receptive and expressive)
   Example: "A baby is little; a man is _____".
   "What is the difference between steel and glass?"
2. Fund of general information (expressive)
   Example: "Why do we wear shoes?"
   "In what kind of store do we buy bread?"
3. Comprehension (expressive)
   Example: "How many pennies make a nickel?"
   "How are a coat and a dress alike?"
4. Vocabulary (expressive)
   Example: Defines words such as *swing, orange, eyelash.*
5. Sentence memory (receptive and expressive)
   Example: "Staying up too late at night can make you very sleepy."
6. Counts items (receptive and expressive)
   Example: "Give me 4 pencils." "Give me 5 blocks."

Nonverbal

1. Skips
2. Stands on one foot 10 seconds or longer
3. Draw a person
   Example: Reasonably good proportion; trunk, fingers, ears, nostrils and feet.
4. Walk backward heel to toe
5. Rides bike
6. Copies □O

SCHOOL READINESS FOR FIRST GRADE

1. Recognizes number units of 2, 3, 4
   Example: Tells how many when appropriate number of paper clips are presented.
2. Knows 8 basic colors

Example: Names color when presented with red, blue, orange, green, white, yellow, black, purple crayons.

3. Knows street address, telephone number, father's first name, occupation
4. Prints first name
5. Identifies most letters of alphabet
6. Prints majority of alphabet (may be reversals)
7. Prints numbers to 10 (may be reversals)
8. Counts to 15 by ones
9. Correctly names a ○, □, and △

AGE 7

Verbal

1. Repeats 5 digits forward (receptive and expressive)
2. Repeats 3 digits reversed or backward (receptive and expressive)
3. Problem solving (receptive and expressive)
   Example: "If one piece of candy costs 3 cents, what will two pieces cost?"
   "How many days make a week?"
   "What are shoes made of?"
   "Why do people work?"
4. Vocabulary (expressive)
   Example: Can define words such as *polite, brave,* and *roar.*
5. Analogy (receptive and expressive)
   Example: "How are a penny and a nickel alike?"
6. Knows right from left
   Example: "Show me your left hand."

Nonverbal

1. Copy a ◇
2. Draw a person
   Example: Now includes clothing, trunk length greater than width, arms and legs in two dimension.
3. Copy a ⌗

Beginning at about this age, the most significant mental development milestones are generally of a verbal rather than non-verbal nature. Academic achievement is an excellent source of developmental information from this age and above, and appropriate academic milestones are listed on the next pages.

FIRST GRADE ACHIEVEMENT LEVELS

Beginning First Grade

(After 3 months in first grade)

Word Recognition	*Reading*
Red	I see a ball.
Come	The ball is red.
Dog	It is big.
Cat	I like to play ball.
See	
We	

Mid First Grade

(After 6 months in first grade)

Word Recognition	*Reading*
Tree	The boy has a dog.
Father	The dog wanted to play.
Chair	He wanted to play on the bed.
House	But the boy said, "No."
Ask	Then the dog went away.
Eat	

End of First Grade

Word Recognition	*Spelling*
Dinner	Go
Breakfast	Cat
Please	Boy
Cover	And
Them	
Dark	

Write from Oral Dictation
I saw the big dog.

Arithmetic
Adds and subtracts digits to 10.
Counts by ones to 100.
Counts by 2s, 5s, 10s to 50.

Knows 47 is bigger than 29.
Tells time to the hour.
Divides paper into fourths.
Knows value of a penny, nickel, dime.

Reading
The children wanted to go fishing.
They were afraid it was going to rain.
But after breakfast the sun came out.
It was a good day for fishing.
Father went fishing with them.

Comprehension
Comprehension may be measured by asking questions concerning the paragraph after the child has read it. Appropriate questions might be, "What did the children want to do?" "What were the children afraid would happen?" "Who went fishing with the children?"

AGE 8

Verbal

1. General knowledge (expressive)
   Example: "How many months are in a year?"
   "Name the days of the week."
   "How many things make a dozen?"
   "Who discovered America?"
2. Likeness and difference (receptive and expressive)
   Example: "How are a nickel and a dime alike and how are they different?"
   "How is a boat and a fish alike and how are they different?"
3. Vocabulary (expressive)
   Example: Defines words such as *school, diamond, infection.*
4. Social judgment (receptive and expressive)
   Example: "What should you do if a boy smaller than you hits you?"

Nonverbal

1. Copy complex spatially integrated designs ⬡◇

2. Draw a person

> *Example:* Quite detailed including neck, fingers, waistline, and complete clothing.

SECOND GRADE ACHIEVEMENT LEVELS
(Mid to end of Grade 2)

Word Recognition	*Spelling*
Does	Cut
Corner	Cook
Turkey	Night
Strong	Dress
Quarter	
Every	

Write from Oral Dictation

The boy had a big cat.

Arithmetic

Adds two-digit numbers, $23 + 14 = \_\_$.
Subtracts two-digit numbers, $39 - 22 = \_\_$.
Writes 435 on command.
Four 2s are $\_\_$.
Which is larger, 534 or 398?
What fraction is one part of 2?
$9 + 4 = 7 + \_\_$.
$11 - 4 = 9 - \_\_$.
Tells time to the half hour.

Reading

The elephant's trunk is used like a hand. Have you ever watched an elephant eat peanuts? He picks up the nuts with his trunk and puts them in his mouth. This is also the way elephants eat hay and grass. When the elephant gets hot he cools off by splashing water on his back with his trunk.

Comprehension Questions

"How does an elephant eat peanuts?"
"What does an elephant do when he gets hot?"

AGE 9

Verbal

1. Repeats 4 digits reversed (receptive and expressive)
   Example: "Say these numbers backward, 4-7-9-2." (2-9-7-4)
2. Gives 3 rhyming words (expressive)
   Example: "Name three words that rhyme with *bat*."
   　　　　　"Name three words that rhyme with *red*."
   　　　　　"Name an animal that rhymes with *hat*."
3. Problem solving (receptive and expressive)
   Example: "If you buy two 4-cent stamps, how much change
   　　　　　would you get back from a dime?"
   　　　　　"If you buy 17 cents worth of candy, how much change
   　　　　　would you get back from a quarter?"
4. Vocabulary (expressive)
   Example: Defines words such as *curiosity, destroy, hero*.
5. Word fluency (expressive)
   Example: "Say as many words as you can think of." (25 in one
   　　　　　minute)
6. Name the 4 seasons of the year (expressive)

Nonverbal

1. Bounce a ball with non-preferred hand
2. Drawings of people should contain action

THIRD GRADE ACHIEVEMENT LEVELS
(Mid to end of Grade 3)

Word Recognition	*Spelling*
Toward	Order
Troublesome	Peach
Provide	Watch
Answer	Enter
Different	
Perhaps	

Write from Oral Dictation
The yellow truck was a funny sight.

Arithmetic

$49 + 37 = $___; $392 + 719 = $___
$283 - 194 = $___; $1432 - 595 = $___

Write 1043 or 2439.

What is 5×9? What is 6×7?

$45 \times 9 = $___; $123 \times 6 = $___
$124 \div 4 = $___; $413 \div 7 = $___

Tells time accurately to the minute.

How many minutes are there in $1\frac{1}{2}$ hours?

$1/3 + 1/3 = $___

Reading

The children went to the zoo on Saturday morning. They saw many different kinds of animals. They enjoyed the clever monkeys the most. It was interesting to watch them peel oranges and bananas. Then they would quickly pop the fruit into their mouths.

The monkeys chased each other around the cage and up and down the tree in the cage. Sometimes they would escape another monkey by swinging from a tree branch using their strong tails. Perhaps they were playing tag.

Comprehension Questions

"Where did the children go?"
"What did the children see?"
"What did the children enjoy most at the zoo?"

For all word recognition items, it is best to show the child words which are all in lower case letters, since mixing capital and lower case letters may be confusing to some children.

BIBLIOGRAPHY

1. Cronbach, Lee J.: *Essentials of Psychological Testing*. New York, Harper, 1949.
2. Ghiselli, Edwin E., and Brown, Clarence W.: *Personnel and Industrial Psychology*. New York, McGraw-Hill, 1948.
3. Hartlage, Lawrence C.: Differential diagnosis of dyslexia, minimal brain damage and emotional disturbances in children. *Psychology in the Schools, IV(1):*403, 1970.
4. Super, Donald E., and Crites, John O.: *Appraising Vocational Fitness*. New York, Harper, 1962.
5. Wechsler, D.: *Wechsler Intelligence Scale for Children*. New York, The Psychological Corporation, 1949.
6. Wechsler, D.: *Wechsler Preschool and Primary Scale of Intelligence*. New York, The Psychological Corporation, 1949.

Appendix A

DISTRIBUTION OF INTELLIGENCE QUOTIENTS

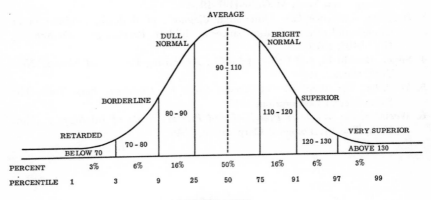

SUMMARY

1. Fifty per cent of all children fall within the average IQ (90-110) range.

2. Twenty-five per cent of all children fall below the 90 IQ level, making them mentally limited for traditional educational programs.

3. Twenty-five per cent of all children fall above the 110 IQ level, making them at least bright normal, or potential college material.

4. IQ <70 qualifies child for educable mentally retarded classes.

5. IQ <55 qualifies child for trainable mentally retarded classes.

Appendix B

CORRELATIONS BETWEEN DEVELOPMENTAL TESTS AND SUBSEQUENT INTELLECTUAL DEVELOPMENT

Test	Age Limits	Age at Binet Testing	Correlation
Gessell	4 wks-6 yrs	Preschool	.50
Cattell	2-3 mos	36 mos	.47
Bayley	1-18 mos	School	.47
Griffiths	1-24 mos	5 yrs	.46
Brunet	1 mo-6 yrs	4 yrs	.34

Note: Although correlation coefficients of around .50 do demonstrate some degree of relationship, predictions based on correlations of this size are of no more use for predicting an individual child's subsequent mental growth than a prediction merely based on his parent's intellectual level.

Appendix C

CRITERIA FOR ASSIGNMENT OF CHILDREN TO SPECIAL EDUCATION CLASSES

Intellectual Criteria (I.Q.)   *Types of Classes*

120-up   Accelerated or Gifted:
> May be self-contained, full day classes for the exceptionally bright child, or the child may be placed in other schools' specific curriculum areas such as science or mathematics for only part of the school day.

90-up   Learning Disabilities or Educationally Handicapped:
> A heterogeneous group of children with various psychological and educational deficits. These children typically possess average or better intellectual potential and normal sensory and physical abilities but require specialized instructional and training techniques. These classes include the dyslexic, dysgraphic, dysphasic, and in some instances, the emotionally disturbed.

55-79   Educable Mentally Retarded:
> Children with mild mental retardation qualify for placement in these special education classes. Academics are taught at the child's individual level of readiness. Junior and senior high school special programming is necessary and usually includes vocational education and vocational rehabilitation.

35-55   Trainable Mentally Retarded:
> Children with moderate mental retardation qualify for placement in these special education classes. Academics are not stressed, as emphasis is directed toward preparation for eventual placement in community sheltered workshops. These children remain dependent as adults.

Lower than 35   Severely and Profoundly Retarded:
> These children do not possess sufficient intellectual

[46]

potential to qualify for public school educational or training procedures. They generally are cared for in community-sponsored programs. Most require institutional care as adults.

Nonintellectual Criteria

Physically Handicapped:

These classes are for children having orthopaedic handicaps or special health problems which preclude regular school placement.

Visually Handicapped:

Children having visual acuity of 20/70 in the better eye after correction, who are able to use vision as the principal means of education are typically placed in partially sighted classes. Children with visual acuity of 20/200 or less who require Braille instruction as the principal means of education are placed in blind children classes.

Deaf or Hard of Hearing Children:

Children having acoustical handicaps requiring acoustical modifications such as carpeted floors, visual aids, and auditory training are placed in these classes.

Multiple Handicapped:

These classes are for children with two or more handicapping conditions which result in complex problems making placement inadvisable in special classes with children having single handicaps.

Appendix D

ROSTER OF SPECIAL EDUCATION RESOURCE PEOPLE BY STATE

Alabama
Faye M. Brown
Chief Consultant and Supervisor
Exceptional Children and Youth
State Department of Education
Montgomery, Alabama 36104

Alaska
W. Russell Jones, Director
Division of Instructional Services
State Department of Education
Pouch F.
Juneau, Alaska 99801

Arizona
Mary D. Robinson, Director
Division of Special Education
Department of Public Instruction
1730 West Adams
Phoenix, Arizona 95007

Arkansas
Tom J. Hicks
Director of Special Education
Division of Instructional Services
Little Rock, Arkansas 72201

California
Leslie Brinegar,
Associate Superintendent
Chief, Division of Special Education
State Department of Education
Sacramento, California 95814

Colorado
John A. Ogden, Director
Division of Special Education
Services
State Department of Education
State Office Building
Denver, Colorado 80203

Connecticut
Francis A. McElaney, Bureau Chief
Bureau of Pupil Personnel and
Special Services
State Department of Education
Hartford, Connecticut 06115

Delaware
John S. Charlton, Director
Division of Pupil Personnel Services
State Department of Public
Instruction
Box 697
Dover, Delaware 19901

District of Columbia
Stanley E. Jackson
Director of Special Education
Department of Special Education
Magruder Building
1619 M Street, N. W.
Washington, D.C. 20036

Florida
Landis M. Stetler, Director
Exceptional Child Education
Florida Department of Education
Tallahassee, Florida 32304

Georgia
Herbert D. Nash, Associate Director
Division of Special Education and
Pupil Personnel Services
State Department of Education
Atlanta, Georgia 30334

Hawaii
Dr. Wayne D. Lance, Director
Northwest Regional Special
Education
Instructional Materials Center
University of Oregon
1612 Columbia Street
Eugene, Oregon 97403

Idaho
Raymond H. Lehrman
Director of Special Education
Instructional Services
Room 206, State House
Boise, Idaho 83707
Robert D. Cain,

Illinois
Assistant Superintendent
Division of Special Education
Services
316 South Second Street
Springfield, Illinois 62706

Indiana
Niles Daggy, Director
Division of Special Education
State Department of Public
Instruction
401 State House
Indianapolis, Indiana 46204

Iowa
Tom Chastain, Director
Special Education Instructional
Materials Center
University of Kansas
1115 Louisiana
Lawrence, Kansas 66044

Kansas
James E. Marshall, Director
Division of Special Education
State Department of Education
120 East 10th Street
Topeka, Kansas 66612

Kentucky
Stella A. Edwards, Director

Division of Special Education
State Office Building
Frankfort, Kentucky 40601

Louisiana
Faye P. McCormick
Director of Special Education
State Department of Education
Capitol Station
P. O. Box 44064
Baton Rouge, Louisiana 70804

Maine
Beverly V. Trenholm, Director
Bureau of Guidance, Special and
Adult Education
State Department of Education
Augusta, Maine 04412

Maryland
Rozelle J. Miller
Coordinator of Special Education
State Department of Education
301 West Preston Street
Baltimore, Maryland 21201

Massachusetts
William A. Philbrick, Jr., Director
Bureau of Special Education
State Department of Education
182 Tremont Street
Boston, Massachusetts 02111

Michigan
Marvin E. Beekman
Director of Special Education
Division of Special Education
State Department of Education
Lansing, Michigan 48902

Minnesota
John C. Groos, Director
Special Education Section
State Department of Education
Centennial Office Building
Saint Paul, Minnesota 55105

Mississippi
Herman K. White, Supervisor

Special Education and Coordinator
Totle VI, ESEA
State Department of Education
Jackson, Mississippi 39205

Missouri
Donald M. Cox, Director
Special Education
State Department of Education
P. O. Box 480
Jefferson City, Missouri 65101

Montana
Roger E. Bauer, Supervisor
Special Education
Office of the Superintendent
of Public Instruction
State Capitol
Helena, Montana 59601

Nebraska
John B. Lamphere
Director of Special Education
State Department of Education
State Capitol
Lincoln, Nebraska 68509

Nevada
Larry Davis, Director
Exceptional Pupil Education
State Department of Education
Carson City, Nevada 89701

New Hampshire
Manfred F. Drewski
Consultant, Special Education
State Department of Education
64 North Main Street
Concord, New Hampshire 03301

New Jersey
Daniel Ringelheim
Deputy Assistant Commissioner
State Department of Education
225 West State Street
Trenton, New Jersey 08625

New Mexico
Darrell Hindman, Director
Divisin of Special Education

State Department of Education
State Capitol Building
Santa Fe, New Mexico 87501

New York
Anthony J. Pelone, Director
Division for Handicapped Children
State Department of Education
Albany, New York 12224

North Carolina
George A. Kahdy, Director
Division of Special Education
State Department of Public
Instruction
Raleigh, North Carolina 27602

North Dakota
Janet M. Smaltz, Director
Special Education
State Department of Public
Instruction
Bismarck, North Dakota 58501

Ohio
S. J. Bonham, Jr., Director
Division of Special Education
State Department of Education
3201 Alberta Street
Columbus, Ohio 43204

Oklahoma
Maurice P. Walraven
Director of Special Education
State Department of Education
State Capitol Building
Oklahoma City, Oklahoma 73105

Oregon
Mason D. McQuiston
Director of Special Education
Oregon Board of Education
Salem, Oregon 97310

Pennsylvania
William F. Ohrtman, Director
Bureau of Special Education
Department of Education
Box 911
Harrisburg, Pennsylvania 17126

Rhode Island
Francis B. Conley, Consultant
Mental Retardation
State Department of Education
Roger Williams Building
Providence, Rhode Island 02908

South Carolina
W. Owens Corder, Chief Supervisor
Program for Exceptional Children
State Department of Education
1000 Bull Street
Columbia, South Carolina 29201

South Dakota
Robert L. Hickins, Director
State Department of Public
Instruction
804 North Euclid
Pierre, South Dakota 57501

Tennessee
Vernon L. Johnson, Coordinator
Special Education
State Department of Education
Cordell Hull Building
Nashville, Tennessee 37219

Texas
Don L. Partridge, Director
Division of Special Education
Texas Education Agency
201 East 11th Street
Austin, Texas 78711

Utah
R. Ellwood Pace, Coordinator
Special Education Programs
Office of the Superintendent
of Public Instruction
Suite 1050, University Club Building
136 East South Temple
Salt Lake City, Utah 84111

Vermont
Jean S. Garvin, Director
Special Education and Pupil
Personnel Services
State Department of Education
Montpelier, Vermont 05602

Virginia
S. P. Johnson, Jr., Director
Division of Elementary and
Special Education
State Board of Education
Richmond, Virginia 23216

Washington
John P. Mattson, Director
Department of Special Education
Office of the Superintendent of
Public Instruction
P. O. Box 527
Olympia, Washington 98501

West Virginia
Roger P. Elser
Director of Special Education
State Department of Education
Charleston, West Virginia 25305

Wisconsin
John W. Welcher, Administrator
Division for Handicapped Children
and Assistant State Superintendent
State Department of Public
Instruction
126 Langdon Street
Madison, Wisconsin 53702

Wyoming
Sara Lyon James, Director
Division of Exceptional Children
State Department of Education
Cheyenne, Wyoming 82001

(The names listed for directors of special education may change from time to time, but in such cases correspondence will be received by their successors or forwarded to the appropriate resource people.)

Appendix E

ROSTER OF STATE CHAPTERS FOR LEARNING DISABLED CHILDREN

Arizona
Robert English
Arizona Association for Children
with Learning Disabilities
P. O. Box 15525
Phoenix, Arizona 85018

Arkansas
Mrs. Richard Newby
Arkansas Association for Children
with Learning Disabilities
Drawer A, Pulaski Heights Station
Little Rock, Arkansas 72205

California
John Robertson
California Association for
Neurologically Handicapped
Children
5708 North Pleasant
Fresno, California 93705

Colorado
Lawrence E. Brady
Colorado Association for Children
with Learning Disabilities
828 Seventh Street
Denver, Colorado 80202

Connecticut
Mrs. Beatrice E. Benton
Connecticut Association for Children
with Perceptual Learning Disabilities
14 Rockwell Place
West Hartford, Connecticut 06107

Delaware
S. Lup Jung
Diamond State Association for

Children with Learning Disabilities
1508 Emory Road
Wilmington, Delaware 19803

District of Columbia
Robert Jackson
Washington, D.C. Association for
Children with Learning Disabilities
627 Allison Street, N. W.
Washington, D.C. 20011

Georgia
Dr. R. Wayne Jones
Georgia Association for Children
with Learning Disabilities
P. O. Box 27507
Atlanta, Georgia 30327

Hawaii
Mrs. Vi Dolman
Hawaii Association for Children
with Learning Disabilities
P. O. Box 10187
Honolulu, Hawaii 96816

Illinois
Mrs. Bert P. Schloss
Illinois Council for Children with
Learning Disabilities, Inc.
P. O. Box 656
Evanston, Illinois 60204

Indiana
Robert H. Yarman
Indiana Association for Perceptually
Handicapped Children
Route 2, Cable Trail
Fort Wayne, Indiana 46805

[52]

Iowa
Val L. Schoenthal
Iowa Association for Children with
Learning Disabilities
5105 Waterbury Road
Des Moines, Iowa 50312

Kentucky
James T. Eisman
Kentucky Association for Children
with Learning Disabilities, Inc.
P. O. Box 7171
Louisville, Kentucky 40207

Louisiana
James Rigsby
Louisiana Association for Children
with Learning Disabilities
719 Texas
Shreveport, Louisiana 71101

Maryland
Jay B. Cutler
Maryland Association for Children
with Learning Disabilities
320 Maryland National Bank
Building
Baltimore, Maryland 21202

Massachusetts
Nancy Brown
Massachusetts Association for
Children with Learning Disabilities
207 Pleasant Street
Marlboro, Massachusetts 01752

Michigan
Mrs. W. E. Hinrichsen
Michigan Association for Children
with Learning Disabilities
P. O. Box 743
Royal Oak, Michigan 48068

Minnesota
Mrs. Keith Slettehaugh
Minnesota Association for
Children with Learning Disabilities
1900 Chicago Avenue
Minneapolis, Minnesota 55404

Mississippi
Fred C. Bradley
Mississippi Association for Children
with Learning Disabilities
P. O. Box 12083
Jackson, Mississippi 39211

Missouri
Mrs. W. Yates Trotter, Jr.
Missouri Association for Children
with Learning Disabilities
P. O. Box 3303, Glenstone Station
Springfield, Missouri 65804

Montana
Mrs. Violet Keuffler
Montana Association for Children
with Learning Disabilities
Box 2563
Great Falls, Montana 59401

New Hampshire
E. M. Still
New Hampshire Association for
Children with Learning Disabilities
118 Donahue Drive
Manchester, New Hampshire 03103

New Jersey
Robert H. Winnerman
New Jersey Association for Children
with Learning Disabilities
61 Lincoln Street
East Orange, New Jersey 07017

New Mexico
Mrs. Virginia Bourque
New Mexico Association for Children
with Learning Disabilities
1906 Amherst, N. W.
Albuquerque, New Mexico 87108

New York
Martha B. Bernard
New York Association for Brain-
Injured Children
305 Broadway
New York, New York 10007

North Dakota
Mrs. R. A. Johnson
North Dakota Association for
Children with Learning Disabilities
210 South 7th
Moorhead, Minnesota 56560

Ohio
Henry Rumm
Ohio Association for Children with
Learning Disabilities
3160 Brandon
Upper Arlington, Ohio 43221

Oklahoma
George Sevier
Oklahoma Association for Children
with Learning Disabilities
3408 Oklahoma
Muskogee, Oklahoma 74401

Pennsylvania
Mrs. Leon Lock
Pennsylvania Association for
Children with Learning Disabilities
Box 664
Allentown, Pennsylvania 18105

Rhode Island
Mrs. Donald Levine
Rhode Island Association for
Children with Learning Disabilities
P. O. Box 6685
Providence, Rhode Island 02904

South Dakota
Dr. James King
South Dakota Association for

Children with Learning Disabilities
809 Kansas City Street
Rapid City, South Dakota 47701

Texas
Joseph B. Hall
Texas Association for Children with
Learning Disabilities
804 Briarwood Boulevard
Arlington, Texas 76010

Vermont
Gerald L. Nadeau
Vermont Association for Children
with Learning Disabilities
24 Southill Drive
Essex Junction, Vermont 05452

Virginia
Dr. Eleanore Westhead
Virginia Association for Children
with Learning Disabilities
P. O. Box 5651
Charlottesville, Virginia 22901

Washington
Vern Bendixson
Washington Association for Children
with Learning Disabilities
9222 183rd Place, S. W.
Edmonds, Washington 98020

Wisconsin
Eli Tash
Wisconsin Society for Brain-Injured
Children
4628 North 70th Street
Milwaukee, Wisconsin 53218

Appendix F

COMMONLY USED PSYCHOLOGICAL AND ACHIEVEMENT TESTS

INTELLIGENCE TESTS

Wechsler Intelligence Scale for Children (WISC)

Individually administered intelligence test comparing ten subjects with age range of seven to sixteen years. Verbal and nonverbal skills are measured. Subtest scatter is useful in differential diagnosis of learning disabilities from mental retardation. Produces verbal, performance, and full-scale IQ scores.

Wechsler Preschool and Primary Scale of Intelligence (WPPSI)

Individually administered preschool intelligence test constructed similar to the WISC, with age range of four to seven years. Also produces verbal, performance, and full-scale IQ scores.

Stanford-Binet Intelligence Scale

The Stanford-Binet is generally the instrument of choice in the evaluation of young children and moderately to severely retarded older youngsters. Based on the mental age concept, the Stanford-Binet classifies intelligence reliably but is not sufficiently sensitive to be helpful in detecting subtle learning disabilities.

EDUCATIONAL TESTS

Wide Range Achievement Test (WRAT)

Grade placement scores and achievement rates of learning in word recognition, spelling, and arithmetic are quickly assessed by this general academic achievement test. Reading comprehension is not sampled.

Durrell Analysis of Reading Difficulty

Complete analysis of the reading process is incorporated, including oral and silent paragraph reading, listening comprehension, phonic skills, and word recognition. Grade equivalent scores are delivered for rate and comprehension.

Spache Diagnostic Reading Scales

Oral and silent reading skills and listening comprehension are measured from grade one through eight.

[55]

LANGUAGE TESTS

Illinois Test of Psycholinguistic Abilities (ITPA)
> The ITPA is a useful instrument in the diagnosis and remediation of expressive and receptive language disorders.

Peabody Picture Vocabulary Test (PPVT)
> Receptive vocabulary development of preschool and school-age children is quickly assessed by this test and offers comparison with expressive vocabulary as measured on most intelligence tests.

Wepman Auditory Discrimination Test
> The Wepman Test measures the child's ability to discriminate the subtle differences between similarly sounding phonemes. Phonic reading instruction may be unsuccessful with children having impairment.

VISUAL-MOTOR TESTS

Bender Gestalt Test
> This is a geometric figure copying test that measures a child's ability to integrate visual perception and motor coordination. Typically employed with children above eight years of age due to the complexity of some of the eight drawings.

Developmental Test of Visual-Motor Integration (Beery)
> Similar to the Bender, this test is appropriately administered to preschool youngsters and delivers an age equivalent of maturation in this area.

Appendix G

REPRESENTATIVE OCCUPATIONAL LEVELS ATTAINED BY INDIVIDUALS OF VARIOUS INTELLECTUAL LEVELS

Intellectual Level	Occupational Level
130 and up (Very Superior)	Senior professional people: Senior executives of large corporations, senior statesmen, senior university professors.
120-130 (Superior)	Professional people: Physicians, accountants, chemists, engineers, dentists, college teachers.
110-120 (Bright Normal)	College graduate level positions: Supervisors, production managers, nurses, school teachers, pharmacists.
100-110 (Normal +)	Skilled tradesmen: Electricians, licensed practical nurses, policemen, machinists, secretaries, opticians, meat cutters.
90-100 (Normal —)	Semiskilled jobs: Firemen, painters, hospital orderlies, carpenters, bricklayers, timekeepers, file clerks.
80-90 (Dull Normal)	Unskilled labor: Miners, truck drivers, factory workers, cooks.
70-80 (Borderline Retarded)	Lower level regular jobs: Dishwashers, domestics, porters, farm workers, laborers.
70-Below	Lower level irregular jobs: Day laborers, migrant unskilled workers, fishermen, sheltered workshop employees.

Appendix H

SAMPLES OF HUMAN FIGURE DRAWINGS OF CHILDREN AT VARIOUS AGES

Age 4

Not human in appearance, Head and one other part required.

Age 5

Human in appear-
ance. Head and
trunk, also arms
or legs and eyes,
mouth or nose.

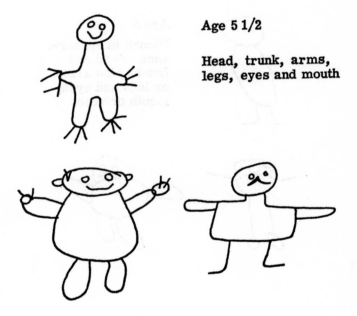

Age 5 1/2

Head, trunk, arms,
legs, eyes and mouth

Age 6

Better proportion
than 5 1/2. Nose
and hair also
present.

Age 6 1/2 - 7

All requirements of
age 6. Also clothing
clearly indicated,
length of trunk is
greater than width,
fingers required.
Sex clearly indicated.

Age 8

Clothing complete, eye detail included, neck is apparent, shoulders are represented, waist required, all lines meet properly.

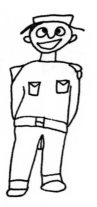

Appendix I

SAMPLES OF COPYING ABILITIES OF CHILDREN AT VARIOUS AGES

Age 3

Age 4

Age 5

Age 6

Age 7

Age 8

Appendix J
SAMPLE PICTURE RECOGNITION TASKS

AGE 2 PICTURE RECOGNITION TASKS. *Chair, Ball, Hat, Key.*

AGE 2 PICTURE RECOGNITION TASKS. *Bed, Cup, Airplane, Telephone.*

AGE 3 PICTURE RECOGNITION TASKS. *Duck, Snake, Elephant, Lion.*

AGE 3 PICTURE RECOGNITION TASKS. *Horse, Bear, Cat, Bird.*

AGE 3 PICTURE RECOGNITION TASKS. *Carrying, Cooking.*

AGE 3 PICTURE RECOGNITION TASKS. *Drinking, Swimming.*

AGE 5 PICTURE RECOGNITION TASKS. *Saluting, Arguing.*

AGE 5 PICTURE RECOGNITION TASKS. *Fighting, Balancing.*

AGE 8 PICTURE RECOGNITION TASKS. *Anger, Sadness.*

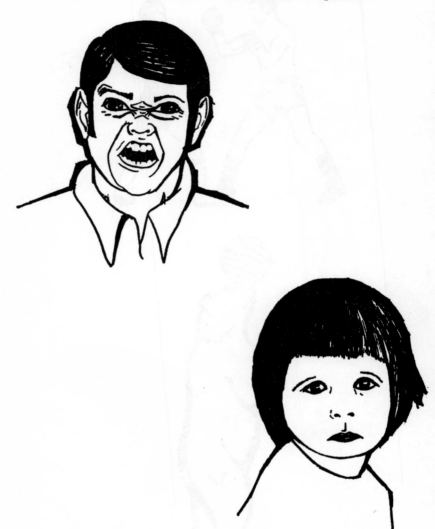

AGE 8 PICTURE RECOGNITION TASKS. *Fear, Happiness.*

INDEX

A

Academic achievement
see School readiness
Activities, recognition, 5, 9
sample pictures, 70-73
Age
Knowledge of own, 9, 35
Levels:
2   4, 31
2½   4-5, 31-32
3   5-6, 32-33
3½   6-7, 33
4   7-8, 33-34
4½   8-9, 34-35
5   9-10, 35-36
6   10, 36
7   10-11, 37
8   11-12, 39
9   12-13, 41
Alphabet, 37
Aphasia, 24, 28
Arithmetic
1st grade, 16, 38
2nd grade, 17-18, 40
3rd grade, 19, 42

B

Binet Test, (Appen. F), 55

C

Categorizing ability, 10, 12
Child psychiatry, 29
Child psychology, 30
College, potential ability, 27
Complex commands, 8, 33-34
Copying abilities, 6, 9, (Appen. I), 64
Counseling, parents, 8, 22, 24, 25, 27
Counting, 10, 16, 18-19, 34, 36-38

D

Definition of words, 10, 12, 36-37

Design copying, (Appen. I), 64
Digit repetition, 5, 32, 37
Discrimination
visual, 34
size, 6, 33
sex, 5, 8, 34-35
left-right, 11, 37
Draw-A-Person (Appen. H), 58
see (specific) Age level
Dull normal, 22-23
classification (Appen. C), 46
occupational level (Appen. G), 57
Dyslexia, 18-19, 23-25, 46
Dysgraphia, 24-25, 46
Dysphasia, 19
Dyspraxia, 24-25, 46

E

Educational placement (Appen. C), 46
EMR (educable mentally retarded), 21
classification (Appen. C), 46
Emotional Disturbance, 29-30, 46
problems, 24, 46
Emotional maturity, 14
Exceptional mental development, 20-25, 46

F

First grade, 15-17, 38-39
Fluency, language
see (specific) Age level

G

Gross motor development, 21
see (specific) Age level

H

Handicapped
intellectual, 21 (Appen. C), 46